SHE-GIANT
IN THE LAND OF
HERE-WE-GO-
AGAIN

Kristina Andersson Bicher

MADHAT PRESS
CHESHIRE, MASSACHUSETTS

MadHat Press
PO Box 422, Cheshire MA 01225

The Library of Congress has assigned
this edition a Control Number of
2020933037

ISBN 978-1-952335-00-6 (paperback)

Cover design by Marc Vincenz
Cover art by Deborah Hake Brinckerhoff
Author photo by Alison Sheehy
Book design by MadHat Press

www.MadHat-Press.com

Table of Contents

The Widow Sings a Love Song

praise the nape of you where
dark bee of my mouth goes troubling
the plum swale   let me sink   through some small bore
into your tiny breathing eden   pluck
every strap and sound every stream
o sweet incandescence I could sculpt
with a spoon

Prophecy (I)

Today, it rained black sand.
—Rev. Jon Steingrimsson, *Fires of the Earth*, 1783

What once was hill, now deep bowl,
where love, split earth. Clouds
lie thick on our tongues. There, the window
where sulfur streams into her bedchamber
and there, the meadow floor where she waits
for him one early June, sun folded into her soft
blond plaits and the weight of her skirts
crushes the wild violets. Her cheek to dirt
to feel for the violence of his approaching
hooves, how her heart bleats blind into the whorl
of her ear, and restless gods gyre beneath the grass.
The widow who worships the Reverend,
here under my foot. And the linen bedding
where she tosses, breathless.

Interregnum; or, Man Caught Between Gods

Wife is white with anger.
For I looked our baby
in the eye
named her *Gudrun*
spoke it aloud and
now
her snow-sleep
deepens.
Tonight, I laid her
under snowdrift
as I was taught *(how
the wind rises)*.
Forgive me:
for eating
we scrape lichen
from trees.
Ancient gods, are you
asleep?
Rise up.
O, Ymir, O Bur.
I am lost.

Unborn

I am mar   scar   flat star

eat and heal
pig's squeal

excise and reveal

I am verve and flash
verse when I slash

hand in flight

I am hack

heft   flesh bereft
lift and lack

precision's scream
base dream

Kirkjubaejarklaustur

This is how you break the children—
This is how you sever the husband—

with ice and flame

take them to the land

of unspeakable names
and beauty
unstoppable

and drop them

in a white one-story hotel where you just enjoyed
a most refined meal:
farm-raised Arctic char
boiled potatoes, peeled
and shaped into elegant, oblong eggs
stitch of dill

the lobby chandelier is modern, glass, and the floors, blond ash
and you drop them
on the heads
of nothing
they dangle in the hallway
and they look at you in disbelief
and they dangle

next day you buy a book from 1783
about nine months
of devastation
sulfur, ash and swollen sheep
here in this small town
where the earth ripped in two
where you left them

Vaðlaheiðarvegavinnuverkfærageymsluskúraúti-
dyralyklakippuhringur

Means key ring of the key chain of the outer door to the storage tool shed of the road workers on the Vaðlaheiði plateau. Specificity does not always help. I cannot find a plateau anywhere. Nor would I recognize the road workers if I ran them over in my rental car. Likewise, the toolshed is a mystery. I am of no use. People will suffer because of me.

Ode to Restraint in a West Village Bar
(Or other gods I have invoked)

Lord, I knew that man was taken but hey—
the Appletini bit my heel and I was hard
with hunger, coiled on a red leatherette
barstool west of Eden. O, praise his teeth, bright
as a life raft, praise his golden throat. How could I
have known that Eros dressed me that morning,
hand-picked the black lace bra. Did someone say
wife? Damn Sophrosyne, muse of duller heads,
I was home free till you showed up, keeping my rosy
fingers off his wine-dark jeans, the meat of his knee. Can't
you see I'm owed? Slither me up the white calf
of Atlas to burn that bright scapula
blade blue. I would rip the sky
to fill my mouth—

How to Get Out of a 20-Year Hole

a prison spoon, sharp teeth, a rosary
and chicken feet, a compass rose, magnetic blood
TNT, equanimity, and a diamond file for a finger;
jeweler's loupe, rubber suit, passport stamp
kick in the ass, the right shoes, the North Star
a shiv and an ampule of musk; sulfuric acid,
wooden mask, litmus test, laughing gas, atom bomb
doctor's note, hammer of Thor, a metaphor,
a stronger rope, a longer hope, a golden tongue
le mot juste, safer roost, divining rod
echolocation and a sleeve of magical staves

But in order to exit, I first had to step over the body

Lament (I)

is there

out there any body
anybodyanybody

hello everything

I have ever done
my body is a field in winter

open to crows

And Eve Knew Even Before

Lord, I can't sleep for fear of my son. I know the rage
of Cain: the blame he hoards, visions that plague, what fevers

him for days, how fire singes night's edge and I cannot sleep
for fear. I can't dream for my son, Lord. I cannot dream to
     dream.

Two small boys on a dust floor; I, the heart of one, mind
of the other. I reap lambs and cold grasses. The black glare

of Cain's eyes and the black back of Abel lifting, sinking,
mine: night without moon. I don't breathe. Hear the night

steps of Cain—how he opens the tent flap and lets the desert in,
a cold roar of stars. War is coming. Lord, close your palm
     around me.

Seal my eyes. Turn me out again, again than to know
what I do. I see sword tips bloom orange at earth's end where
     you

left me. Remember when we met? It was a Saturday. Remember
how I swayed for you under trees?

Kristina Andersson Bicher

Advice of the Father

keep all

as whatever

as therefore

not to be with

no, but for the fullness

On Visiting My Brother in Jail

His body built for breaking
      not flight
           spring   unsprung

Bringing Him Home

Because it would crush a woman to bear alone
this time when we pick him up it's Mama
who remembers to buy shoelaces.

Because each of us is only so deep, my sister
this time will open the bowl of her hands
as the doctor crumples scripts into her palm.

Nurses steer him out by his elbow. Our brother,
Superman. The sky is Arizona wide
and cloudless azure and it burns from the inside.

And this time, I wait on black asphalt
in a sea of shined-up cars. A pillar of hot sand.
He comes out through glass front doors

and into the light like a dazzled prize
fighter, instinctively, he ducks—
my fists thicken. His feet have forgotten

how to wear people shoes. We drive home past
a regiment of saguaro cacti. With needled fingers
they salute us. Faceless. Filled with rain.

Eve Dreams

her son is a child
in the desert
has no skin
is lonely
and no longer hers

Missing

After leaving my brother in the mountains, we drove
          together back to separate homes,
my ex-husband and I. Passed signs for caves. Caves inside
          other caves,

a chain of holes beneath us, this road we drove once a dark sea.
          We passed
Antietam, too, and because I like to hear him explain things,
          I ask

what happened here. He knew I would forget, just like the
          Battle of Midway
that he explained to me every single time I walked into his
          favorite movie.

This man who bought me an expensive watch, right after I lost
an expensive watch. I see now how this was love. We left my
          brother Krister

behind, which is also love, I tell myself. I don't feel so good,
          was the last thing
Krister said. My ex is laying out Civil War tactics and I'm
          thinking about

the cows. On the drive down, whole battalions of cows
          scrubbing bare the hills
and now only fields of fog. They had to be somewhere. I
          waited

for a black head to pierce the whiteness as confirmation, like
a sudden musket
flash. Waited. They lost all sense of reality, my ex went on,
what with

the spew of guns and horse guts, roar of bodies torn. Couldn't
tell
enemy from brother. The cornfield was a vast altar, boys buried

where they fell. I realized it had been dark for some time and
we had stopped
speaking. Still so far from our homes, this car a disappearing
light. Someone

turned on the radio and we listened to comedy, the punch
lines coming rapid-fire,
words caustic and crude. Drove and drove for hours, our
laughing relentless.

In the Garden of Mental Illness

Dinner is potluck.
The homecoming has cameras in it.
The mothers wear large sunglasses and parrots
    roost in the chinaberry tree.
The sisters are beautiful and their bright
    teeth carve up the dark.
The biggest man is also the most sad.

Friends come with cards and casseroles and then
    they stop coming.
People speak of earthquakes.
People comment on your shoes because everyone
    is looking down.
Shoelaces are not allowed.
Ditto leather belts.

Cacti pierce the sky.
California is cloudless and fat oranges wobble
    on soft stems.
Pills smell like jasmine.
Nothing is forgotten.

Irony is a luxury.
Human sounds are drowned
    by birds.
Parrots are winged flowers.
The sun keeps burning into our heads.
The saddest woman laughs the loudest.

House by the Road

Our mother told us that if the headlights
which, nightly, swept the blackened
bedroom walls, were to halt—
to stall and hover above your pillow, throw
their halos over your bed, your head, you
would be taken in your sleep that night,
you would not wake again.
And dark shapes fell from the velvet
of the open closet and dark swells pulsed
the seams around the doors and the deep well
under the bed lapped the coverlet hem
and we lay still, quiet and small.
As a child at night in bed, there was only
the heat of brown bats beating, the ring of heels
receding down the hall, the prayer of legs
under the sheet, and the tangled animal
of one's own heart.

The Ring

I'd never touched one

        lifted to light   a telescope
        held low   a jeweler's loupe

     *   *   *

I slid it down my cool finger

        liquid loose   at eight
        built only of hunger   lies

Reading the Ruins

Marriage is a lamentation to the clouds.
Love is the adornment of ships.
You are the spine of a wave.
I am an abode of mortification.
Estrangement is the abomination of the shepherd.
Trust is the augmentation of the earth.
You are a disease fatal to children.
I am a cold grain, also known as the Lord of Valhalla.
Sadness is the toil of the steed.
Fear is the leavings of the wolf.
Comfort is a god with one hand.
Divorce is the pickaxe of the doomed.

Based on the Icelandic Rune Poem.

Kristina Andersson Bicher

Driving in Heat

My heart is glass
is brick
is glass.

And how do we stop this shouting.

Flower Girls

In satin feet, they toe
past our bed, while I sleep; more,

then more, a troupe,
they process in quiet

cobbled to each other, in flesh-
like dresses, girls bound

at the wrist with grosgrain,
soft buttons

of their mouths sewn to buds.
They come at night

the color of muscle, pupils
dilated like prey, they tremble

their faces and hold
their weight in silk

ringlets of vine
pinned silver to their scalps

their hands are posies
bunched in prayer

they do not speak, but oh
but oh—

The Weight of Myth

The brass on their fingers, audacious.
We walked on boiled mud.

The earth opened around my husband's sandal.
There was a wound in the earth and he stepped right into it.

Welcome to the land of here-we-go-again.
At the end of the first saga, a she-giant falls through grass

to the bottom of everything.
There you will find a sour yellow sea.

All over the past we walk without thinking.
Step on everything without even knowing.

Kristina Andersson Bicher

Prophecy (II)

[an erasure from the Book of Isaiah]

Sin heaping children
             upon children.

Utterly, I call: go now, useless.
             Weep no help.
       Rain will soil.
             Walk in it.

Towers fall every hill.
             Bruises he inflicted.

Wrath, tongue
       consuming, rising
             sieve of destruction,
                   jaws astray.

Anger, cloudburst.

Woodcutter's Wife

Is she happy?
Why does she run from me into trees?
Why does she bury her dolls?
Why does she pin her eyes to the sky?
Why does she cut herself with sticks, at night, in bed
        and the blankets
    are spotted dark and I wash and I wash?
Why does she try to clean herself with leaves?

What is to be done with him?
Why does he hide my paring knife?
Why does he fill my shoes with stones?
Why does he sit on my lap, now at 12, and stroke my cheek
    and braid my hair?
Why does his skin always smell though I use my best lye?
Why does he steal his sister's bread?

Husband, dearest, where do you go?
How far do you roam to look for wood?
Why has your axe blade grown dull?
Why do you return after dark and bring home the forest's
        silence in your eyes?
Why do you ask if I'd like meat, perhaps a fat ham, when
        you know I could live on your love?
Why do you furrow and torture your thumbnail?
And what have you done with the children?

City Where the Old City Stood

The fathers are burning the fields and flooding the forests
      they will make a new city where the old city stood

The mothers are the undead   you can dig them out of the
      fields where they live like potatoes

This might be my last radio transmission to you   I might
      not make it back from the future

I'm sorry the mothers are gone   you'll have to speak to the
      fathers

The fathers will chop their way into brightness and the
      mothers' organs are made of moss   the fathers will
      chop wood and the mothers will eat their own moss
      with tiny knives

Gudrun, Morning

And soon her son, disfigured
by woes and so wept over,

will rise. Already sun strikes
his window, the wind-up clock

a carcass split on the sill,
spilled gold gears and brass screws.

Toppled wooden town, cows and soldiers
sideways on the circus rug. Soon

he will blink back the last bits
of dreams and launch his long arms.

She sleeps the sleep of seas.
Wakes on her knees.

Kristina Andersson Bicher

Sugar for Krister

because my heart is sloppy

and slow to learn and my mouth
too small to say

what needs to be said

I will buy a pastry
for my brother

in his Bellevue hospital bed

I am the one
who brings Baked Alaska

to the apocalypse

and this my oblation
to the inscrutable god

of genetic misfortune

let me tell you
the story of sugar, how

it is burned

and whipped and still grateful
how it is crushed

and still shines

Kristina Andersson Bicher

After the Fire

goodbye to the maps
we'd fallen in love with

the habitual hills

yes, of course, there was pain—
the constellation

we're born under: isn't our

remaking always
violent,

but look: now the burnt tufts

of hair are virgin forest
a mountain range has bloomed

from my temple to my jaw

ropey and smooth
and now a river like a root

shoots down your neck

into the roiled valley
of your clavicle

a new continent broken

from my back, pink and pricked
with stars

First Night

all dark gesture and whatever ghosts

night holds the voices

the bed waits

shake out the quilt of what remains

and snow comes through the ceiling

Prayer

Mother, today I met a man.

We drank chocolate in the square. He showed me his drawings.
Then he led me to the farthest wood to meet an old friend.
It was a tree. Mother, he was lonely. He had a penknife and
I found a stick and the mountain watched and said nothing.

I dreamt I was a large spoon racketing the walls of an empty
tin pail.

Mother, there is no sign of disease yet all these warnings.

All night roosters keen and the churches won't stop belling.
All night the dogs despair, cry out from one to the next, until
they have strung a net of worry over us all. I pull shut the
curtains and still the mountain sees.

Mother, they say you must ask the mountain permission. The
people throw small lights at its feet and bright tiny flags.

If the mountain were just one man, I would beat it with a
stick.

Mother, I'm not myself. On the first day, a volcano sank into
my eye. On the first day, I made a small church of my tears.

I bought gold shoes so I might fly.

He was a penknife, I was a stick, Mother, was he so lonely? The men call the mountain beautiful. The women quiver, sometimes.

I dreamt a feather flew under my door. The beer ran black and I ate with strangers. And when I screamed, paper flowers grew from out my mouth.

It goes like this with mountains, with men: he rises, I sink.

Mother, when I sleep, the mountain takes a step closer.

I don't sleep, Mother. All night the cats lament in the street, they lament. Their throats are knotted grief.

Mother, today I met a man ...

Lament (II)

We were on a cliff we couldn't see the edge of: naked
on night-grass, I on my right side, he on his back.
I fed him jam pie salted with the ocean's white noise.
A rose-tide above and the voices of stones
buried beneath. Wild stars of white aster sprang
from our feet. *Sub rosa amo. Once we get off this island*
we will never speak.

One Year In

His ambivalence and my ambivalence meet in a coffee shop
on the Upper East Side.
We conclude our exes should get together.
The Triple Ginger scones with plum we once loved are now
too rich.
He continues to talk in circles.
I do nothing to improve my life.
I still come to him with the hunger of a junkie.
Our night-dreams are kaleidoscopic and encyclopedic.
It has become impossible to sleep without his hand on my
belly.
Our goals are not only divergent but wholly antithetical.
Jamaica is the new Iceland.
My breasts are still perfect.
I take him sailing.
He takes me to Lars von Trier's *Nymphomania Vols. I and II.*
We invent new ways to distrust each other.
More women enter our bed.
There is talk of Botox.
I buy him heatproof spatulas; he buys me handmade paper.
He's gained weight since we met. I think this means he's
happy.

In New York

It's raining concrete.

*

I bite down on my grief wetly.

*

Who will test these chains?

*

Improbable escape!

*

Shall we play in the woods?

The Widow Plants Daffodils

When you first tear open the brown paper sack
and peer down, don't be alarmed at their nakedness,
how they huddle in clutches of six or twelve, some
with brittle skins, others bald, and all blank-faced.

Take them one by one, hold each in your palm,
the cream-white meat of its flesh neither heavy nor light,
its body a teardrop with roots.

Then choose a spade, edged with teeth, and cut a hole
twice-deep as they are tall. And among grubs and glass bits,
make for them soft brown caves and line these with bone dust.
Then bury them.

But you won't dream of their slender necks rising, the ruched
cloth of them, all that perfume spilt from loose cups. No,
when cold clamps down around the house, you will stiffen:

shovel the walk and take out the trash in the dark. Trudge
under black bones of trees, try to dislodge
from your mind the difficult man who left in late August
and your grown children gone.

You'll forsake the humble onions that you entombed.
But they, of whom you have asked the impossible,
will not fail you. So stop now, before you begin,

and take a moment to know their names: *Salome, Ice Queen,*
Rip Van Winkle, Early Bride.

Kristina Andersson Bicher

In Order for These Men to Die

He who knew their purpose only too well drove with volcanic fire this comradely pair thence, making them the first to leave, putting an end to their conspiring and cohabitation.
—Rev. Jon Steingrimsson, *Fires of the Earth,* 1783

God, on a fine June day,
chased two men
from the pasture
of their bliss
roof seeded with wild thistle—
unsprung a buried volcano
mountain as hired gun
as blunt instrument—
the damage
was vast.
The land broke red
into living rivers
sky bloomed black
and deep pockets of the earth
sang with the effort.
It was only right.
I fear for my flock.
Self-doubt's
the center's churn.
Hope's sky-high
and pockets of stone—
mountain as failed attempt
at flight. Two men met

in the spring, fell in love:
caught in a sudden bath
an onslaught of blossoms
face first.

Kristina Andersson Bicher

She-Giant

I am the Next-Big-One-
to-Blow. My body
over these seething
fields; no joke, I bear
char marks, black
feather scars.

From Her Diary

He asks if I like it, being slapped
like that, *does it make you hot?*
I say *yes. Yes,* like that
so he must choose how hard
he wants to believe my answer.

But this body sparks:
when my flesh enters
the cup of his hand,
it bites back, his bent arm begs
its own forgiveness.

Or is it my permission that devastates?
He says harder, I say *yes.*

Kristina Andersson Bicher

Woman, Cooking

He is five days
gone and far.
An anvil has formed
dark in her hollows, sunk
into rib and wet lung,
crushing into the flint
of her hips. The body
closes around it.

With her large-tined fork
cow bones
are moved around the iron
pot, slick with oil
and stout; bay leaf. Fists
of meat bronze
and sweeten then
relinquish.

There is No Sun

but what you say is
I have lain

walked through
memorized each

and when you take it
nothing

Kristina Andersson Bicher

The Famine That Follows

We die not
  from fire
    but its quenching—

the flames set down,
  then a barrenness

    our tongues a thick bulb
    a memory of water
    our hungers hoarded
      in the throat

          we will fall
      upon each other
          with forks
            and fingers

we will eat our very names

Then

when you are gone, for good
from me, irrevocably gone,
irretrievable

and when my body has done the brute work
gut and lungs, mouth and fingers
whose very nature is to take
and to hold
and to take
when this same body has put down
its own heat
and turned to feed elsewhere

when I am sitting in my little yellow room
and leaves slipping
inside me
and you, vanished

what will become of you then?

will you be thin lace
fronting the pane
that I can see through but that
alters everything

will you be sun-dust risen
from nowhere, insubstantial
dissolving in shade
that cannot enter me

or will I burnish our story into myth
harden you to marble
will I put you on a horse?

In My Mother's House

O crisping
of cloth! O steamy sighs of irons!

Dear Mother, I cannot

work your loom. My fingers
at the tissue of dreams.

Ephemera

a cello's voice rises up the stairwell

Russians just dug up more ancient birch bark scrolls

send me a shirt towel trousers reins wrote a man called Onus
If I am alive I will pay for it

because of the wind the dog barks   because of the wind
         a child's scream
                  from a far-off swing-set lodges
        in the upper echelons of the oak

sunk in bogs   scrolls under roads in Novgorod
       marry me I want you you want me says Mikita
       to Anna

at the center of the Milky Way   a dormant black hole

Onfim draws an ugly creature *I, beast*

a son opens cupboards   removes two plates

a girl somewhere takes pills   gloss-blue oval
                                        emerald-and-white
        gel capsule

        such a fine world today   says a voice on a machine
        I hope you get out

                        there is coffee in the air

Antietam (I)

Krister is a ghost. We left
him in the mountains. Friends and
doctors assured us of our
rightness so we left him. In
a hollow, amid red hills,
a porch-swing swings, empty and
Krister is sitting on it.

*

Sitting on it a ghost we left
mountains friends and us of our
we left him in amid red hills
swings empty and sitting on it
Krister is him in the doctors' rightness
so a hollow a porch swing
Krister is.

Prophecy (III)

The night the child was made
    was starless
        widow Gudrun's braid
            slapped
            and slapped her back
                  until he unbound it.

~a strange bird, red and green
~the noise of bells from underground
~streams carried sea monsters
~lighting struck a newborn lamb

The Hand of the Maker was Everywhere.

And sinners beware.

The Sister's Elegy

The boy who couldn't wait
to reach our father's height
hits the six-foot mark
on the mug shot.

The thinking went thus:
a young man needs
a proper suit upon reaching
a certain age and so a tailor

was brought in with wooden sticks
and pins to take the full
measure of him. Starched
cuffs and collar held him

in his skin, flag of rainbow silk
and wing tips on his toes,
who knew? He might be
asked to interview for a

white shoe firm. He might be
someone's best man.
Today my brother goes to jail.
Did I just say that?

Did you hear me?

Weight of Myth

falling,
falling
is there room
on my back
for one more

The Mothers Speak to Gods & Giants

We will rake
the sea bottom
for the fallen.
We are a comb
to pull water into strands,
a slotted spoon.
Our legs are tree trunks,
our locked arms chain link.
We are a seine net
of the finest filament.
We are cheesecloth
swept through broth.
We are paper dolls, cut
in accordion folds, sharing one hand
one hip—
we buckle the breeze.

Sub Luna Vivo

after Erik Axel Karlfeldt

I am owed carnage
   jagged.

  Engines gallop
      toward this short-lived
         moon of moats.

  So blue now, I go—

         in surges, in
                rock tides.

Acknowledgments

Poems from this manuscript have been published in the following journals with possible modifications and/or different titles.

Barrow Street: "Unborn" (as "Knife") and "Gudrun, Morning" (as "Morning Prayer")

Bellingham Review: "House by the Road"

Columbia: A Journal of Literature and Art: "Flower Girls" and "Bringing Him Home" (as "Bringing Our Brother Home")

Columbia Journal: "Kirkjubaejarklaustur," "In Order for These Men to Die," and "Woodcutter's Wife"

Crab Creek Review: "Reading the Ruins" and "In the Garden of Mental Illness"

Denver Quarterly: "City Where the Old City Stood" and "After the Fire"

Grist: "Sugar for Krister" (as "Sugar for Stuart")

Hayden's Ferry: "Fasting" (as "Cuba [1993]")

LIT Magazine: "The Famine that Follows"

Narrative: "In New York" and "The Widow Sings a Love Song" (as "Love Song Full of Holes")

Painted Bride Quarterly: "Missing"

Plume Poetry: "Prayer" (as "Woman, Man, Tepoztlan") and "Ode to Restraint in a West Village Bar"

Tupelo Quarterly: "If We Arrive Late to Sunset" and "Lament (II)" (as "Aquinnah Sub Rosa")

Under the Volcano Anthology (Fondo Editorial del Estado de Morelo, 2018): "The Sister's Elegy" (as "The Mother's Elegy"), "Woman, Cooking," and "Antietam (I)" (as "Antietam")

Women's Studies Quarterly: "In My Mother's House"

Women's Voices for Change: "The Widow Plants Daffodils" (as "How to Plant Daffodils")

Zócalo Public Square: "Ephemera"

ABOUT THE AUTHOR

KRISTINA ANDERSSON BICHER is a poet and translator living in New York. *She-Giant in the Land of Here-We-Go-Again* is her debut full-length poetry collection. Her chapbook *Just Now Alive* (FLP, 2014) was a finalist for the New Women's Voices prize. Her translation of Marie Lundquist's *I Walk Around Gathering Up My Garden for the Night* will be published in 2020 in a bilingual edition by Bitter Oleander Press.

Her poems, translations, essays and interviews have been published in *Ploughshares, Colorado Review, Hayden's Ferry Review, Narrative, Barrow Street, Painted Bride Quarterly, The Atlantic, Plume, Brooklyn Rail,* and others. She attended the Bread Loaf Translation Conference and earned degrees from Harvard University and Sarah Lawrence College.

CPSIA information can be obtained
at www.ICGtesting.com
Printed in the USA
FSHW011203300320
68622FS